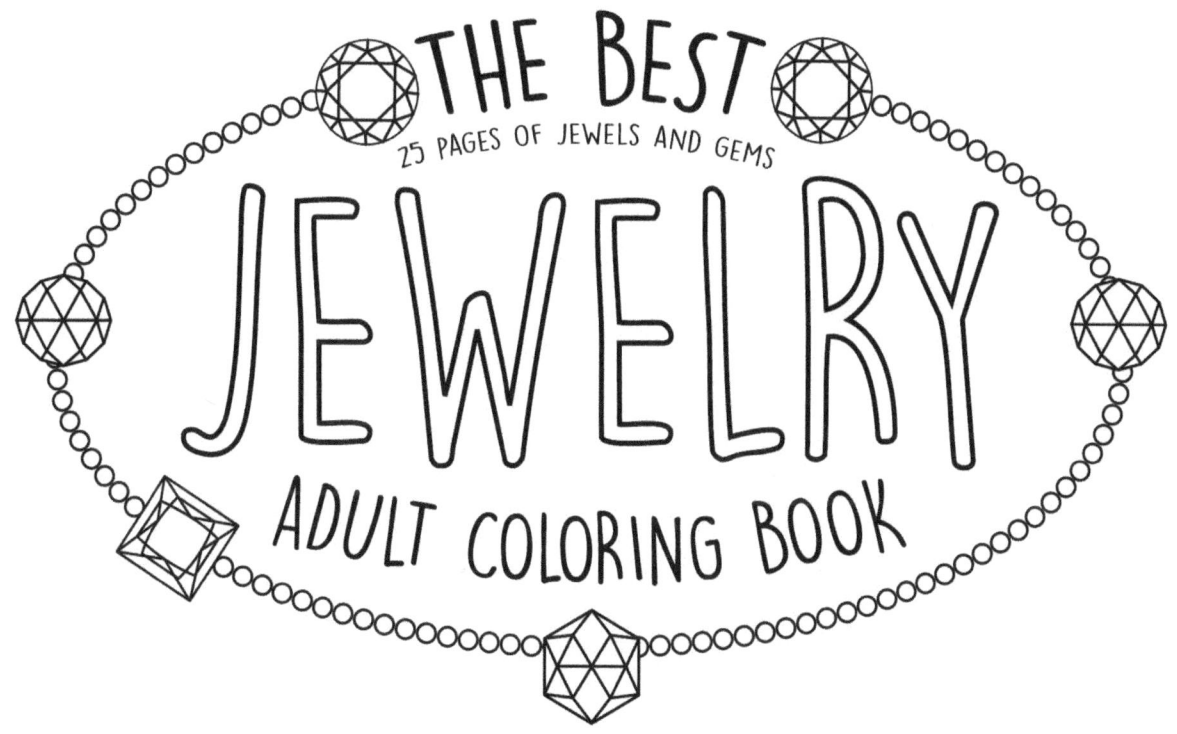

THE BEST

25 PAGES OF JEWELS AND GEMS

JEWELRY

ADULT COLORING BOOK

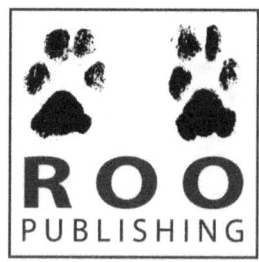

ROO
PUBLISHING

ILLUSTRATED BY DANI KATES

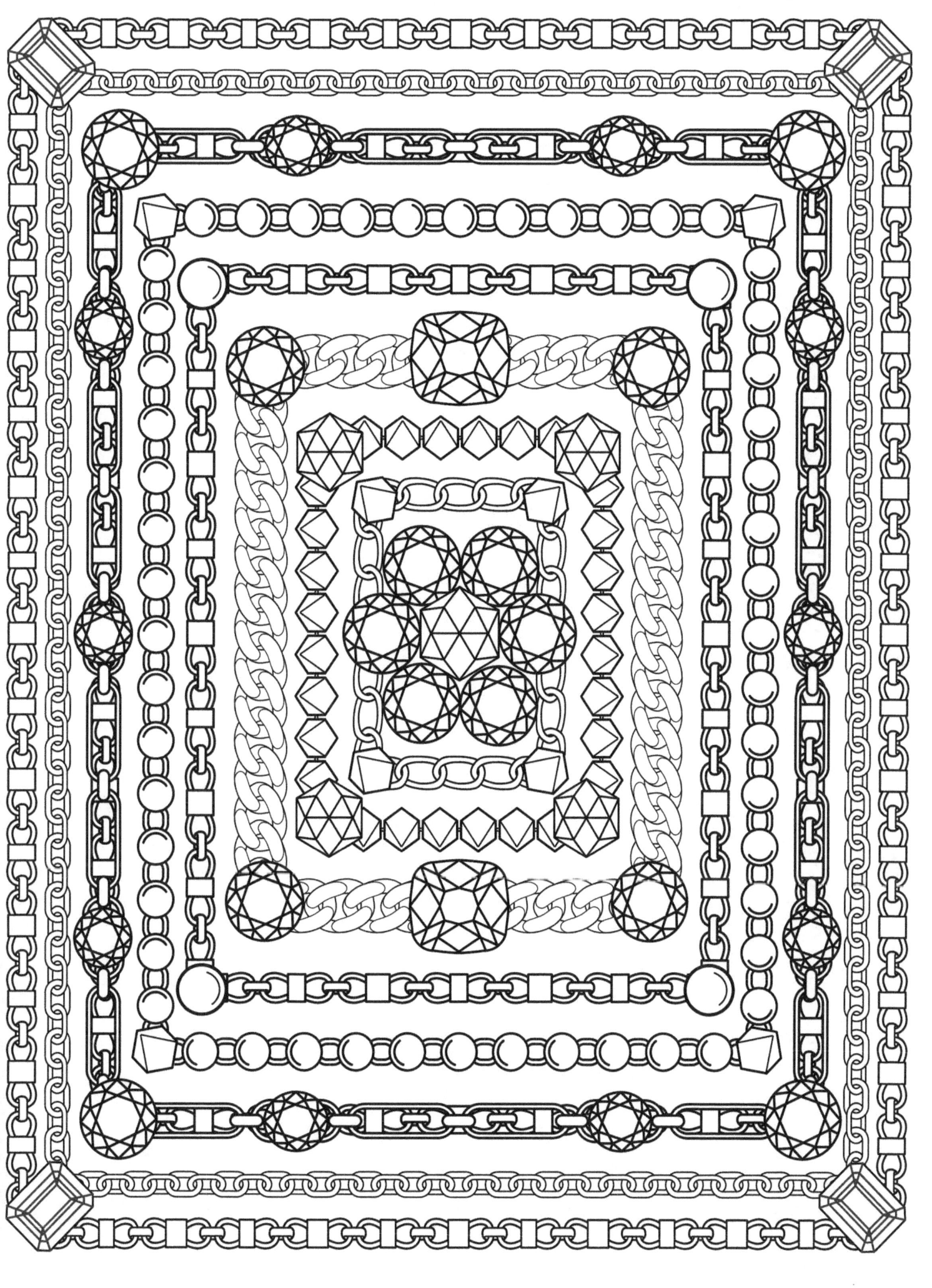

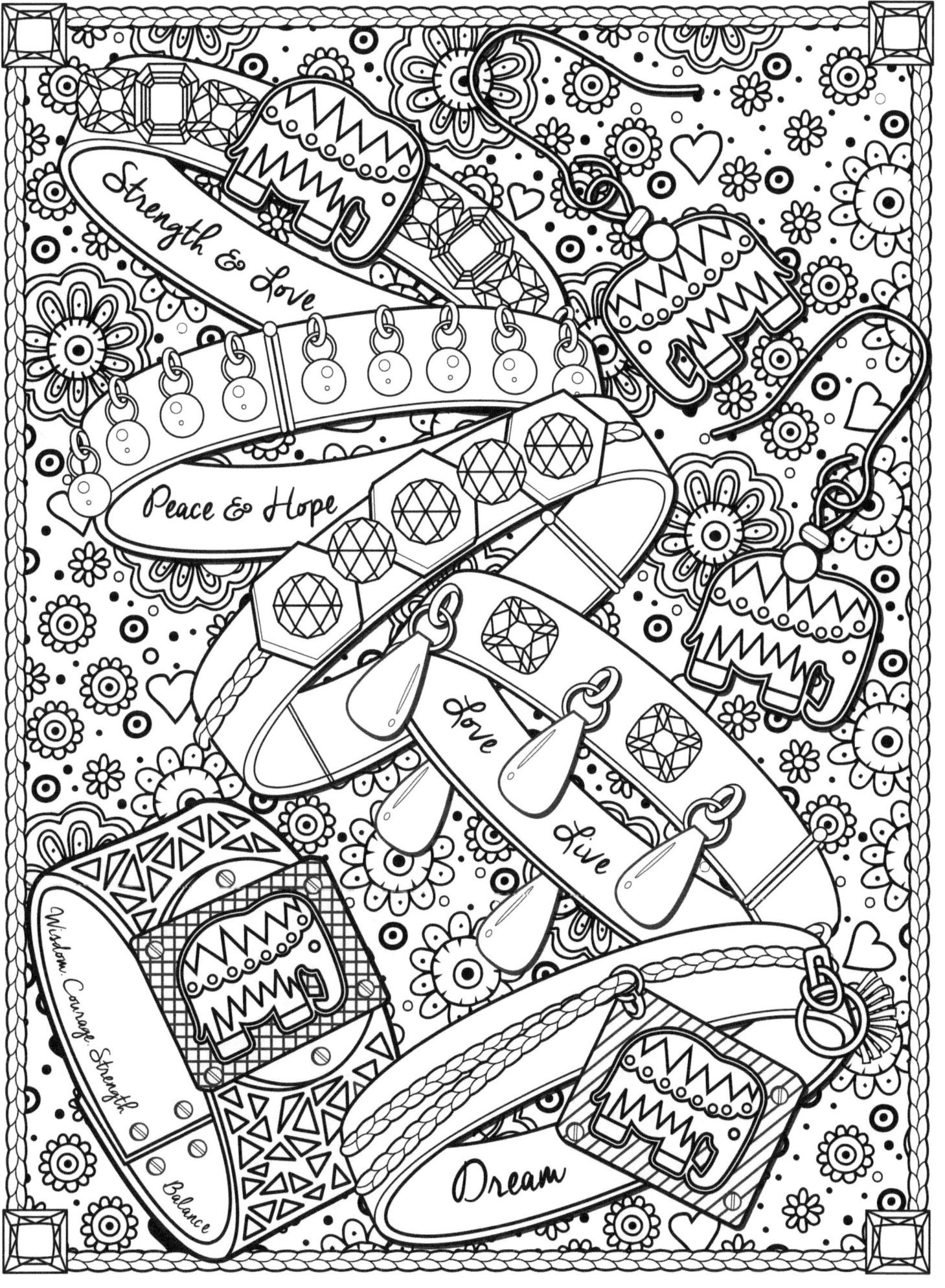

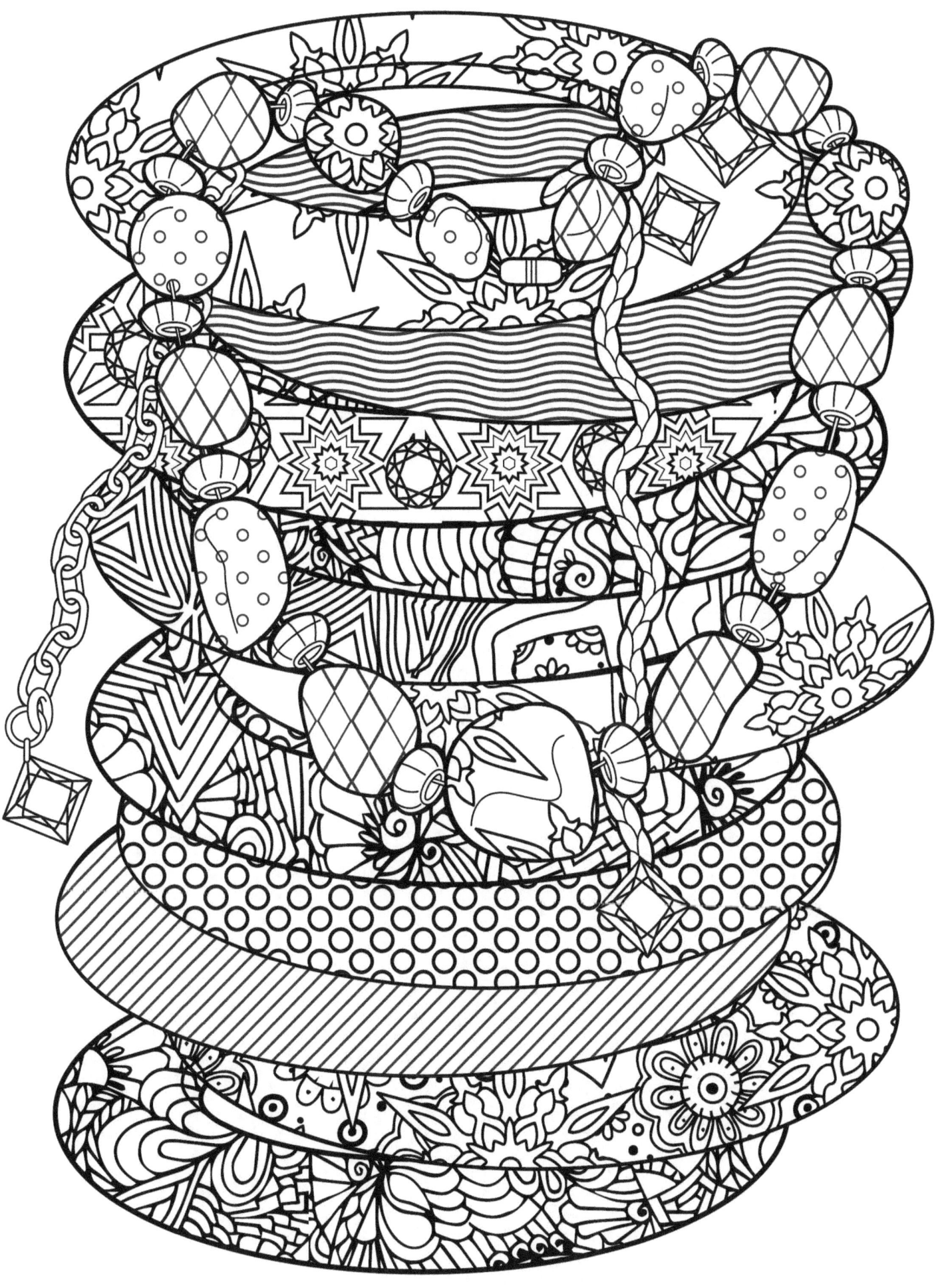

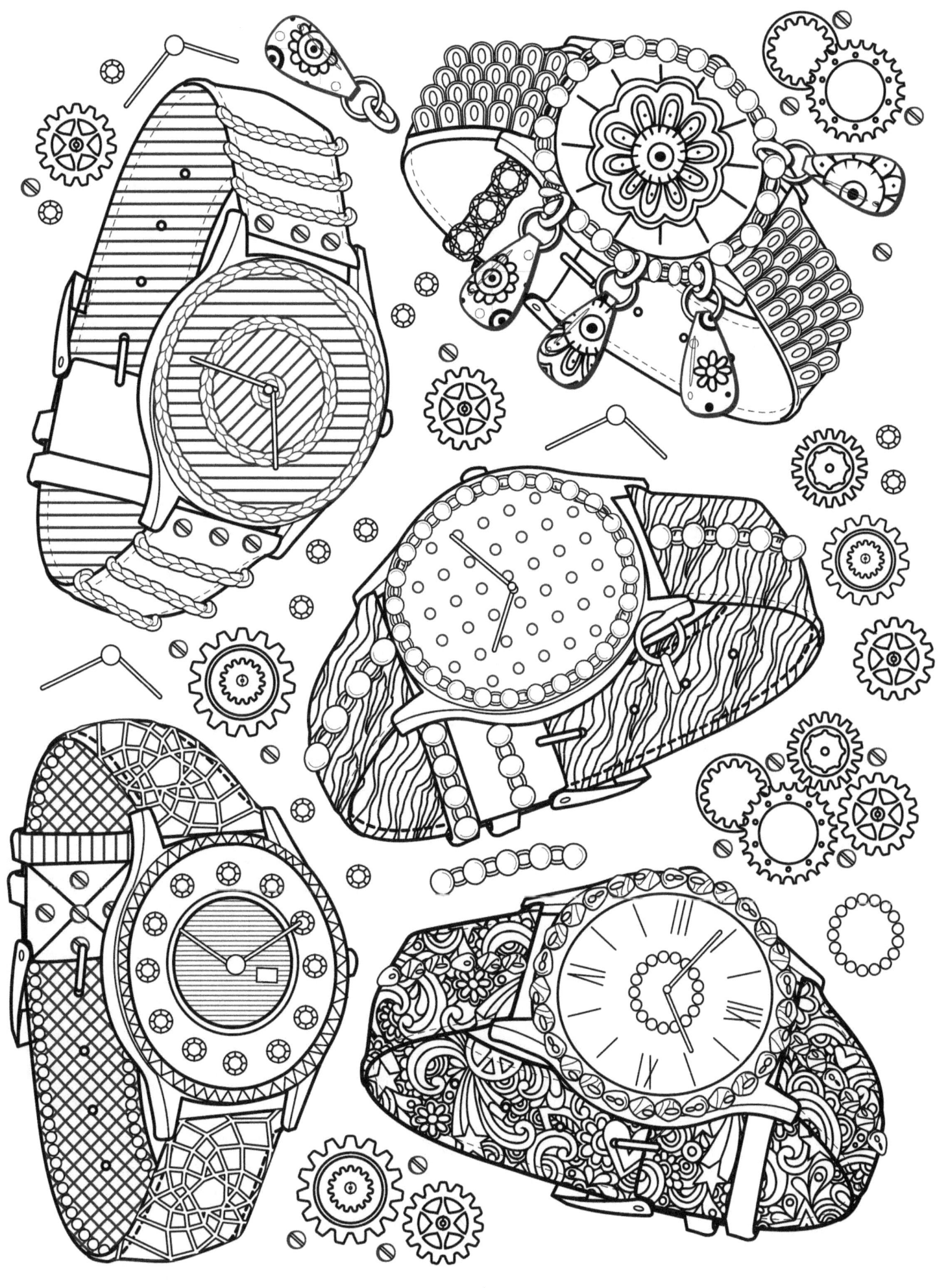

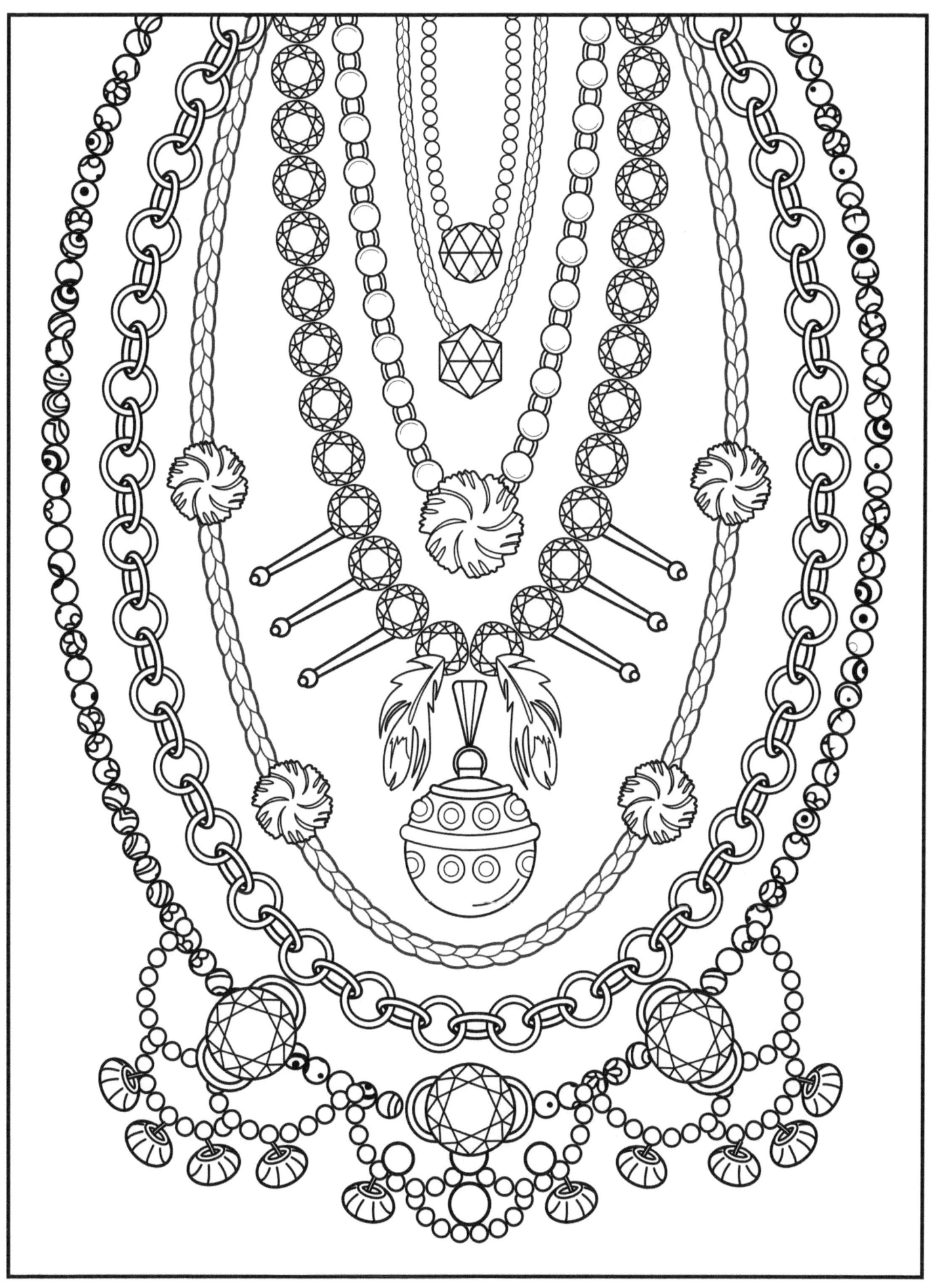

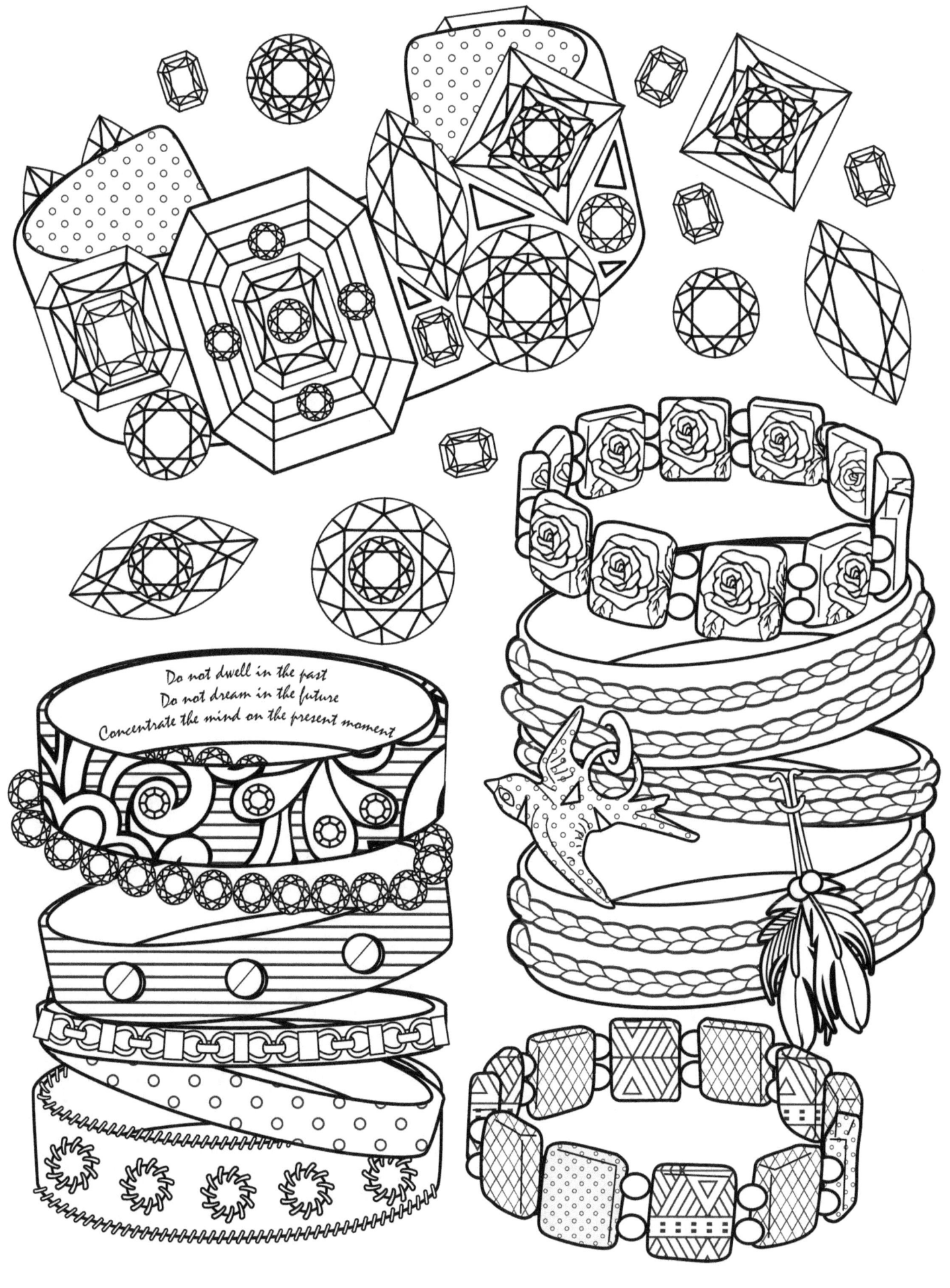

Do not dwell in the past
Do not dream in the future
Concentrate the mind on the present moment

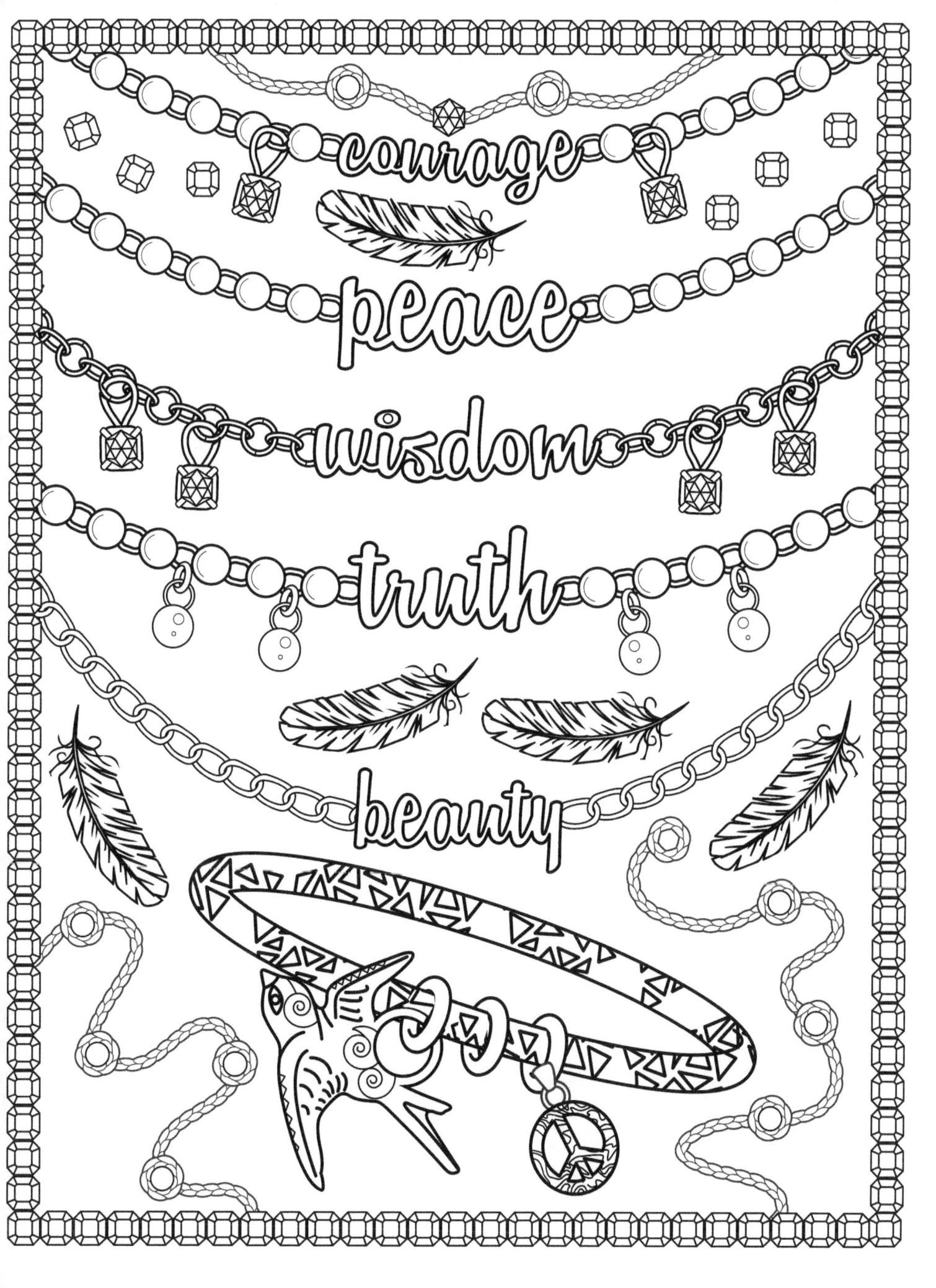

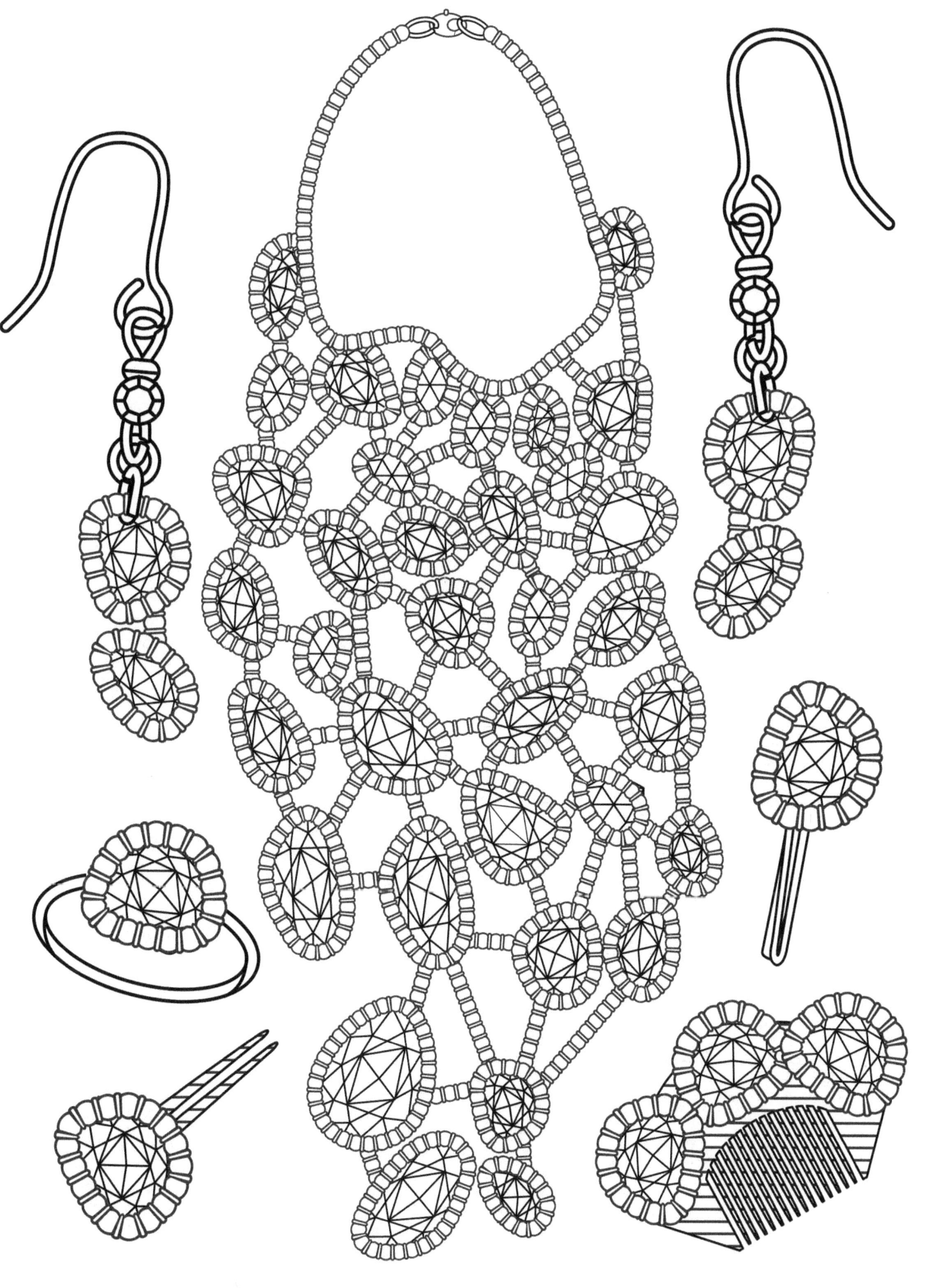

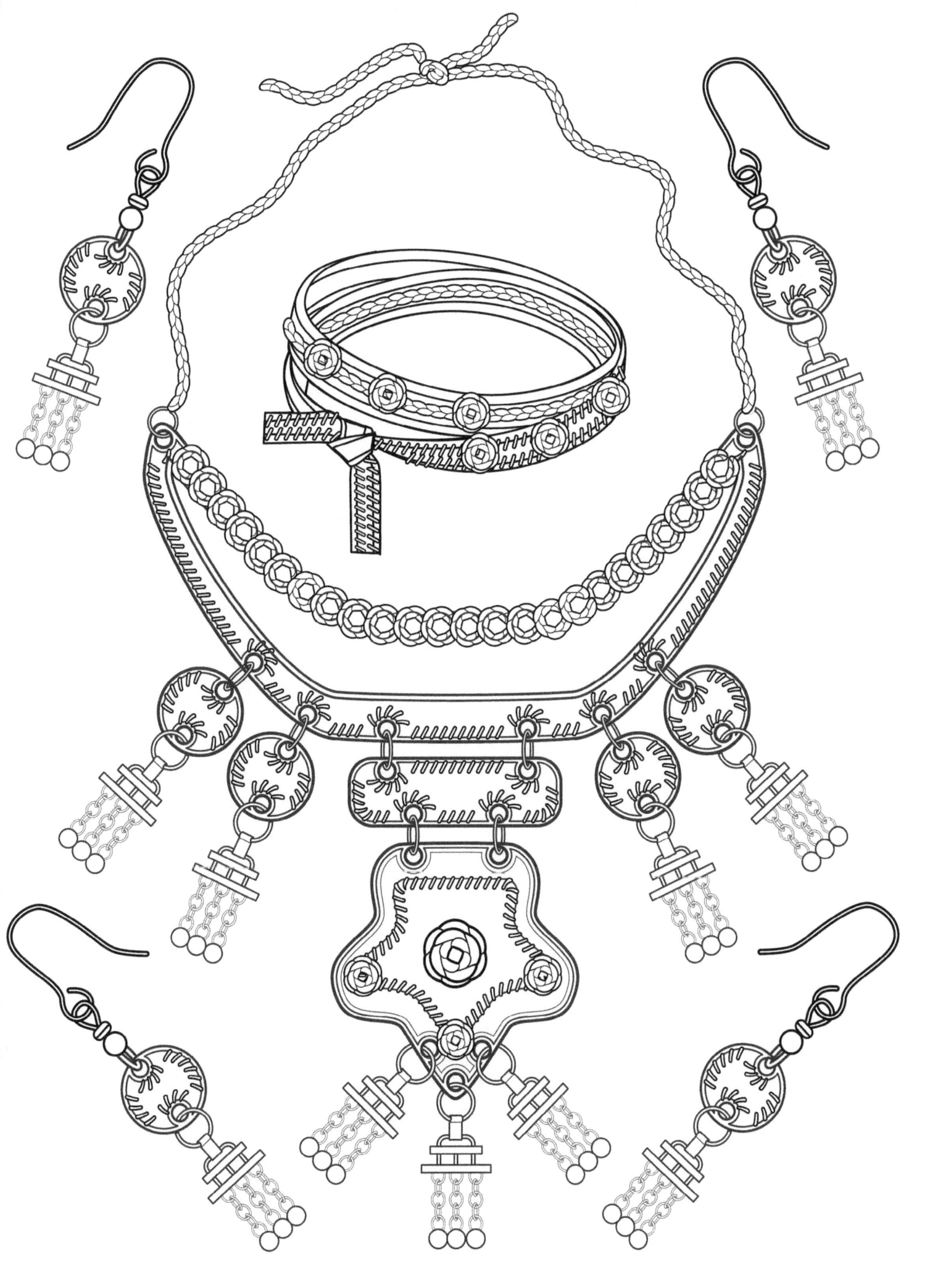

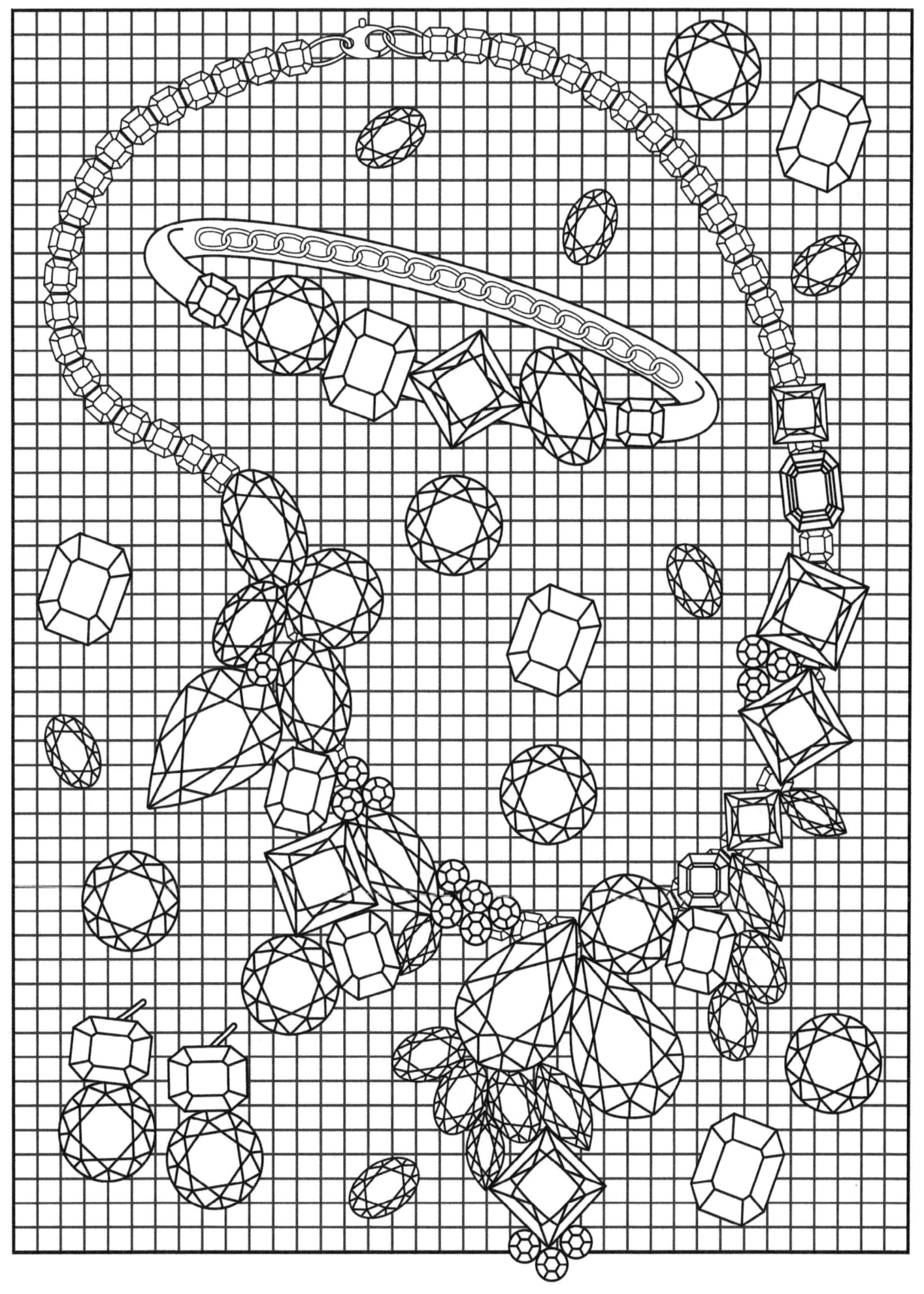

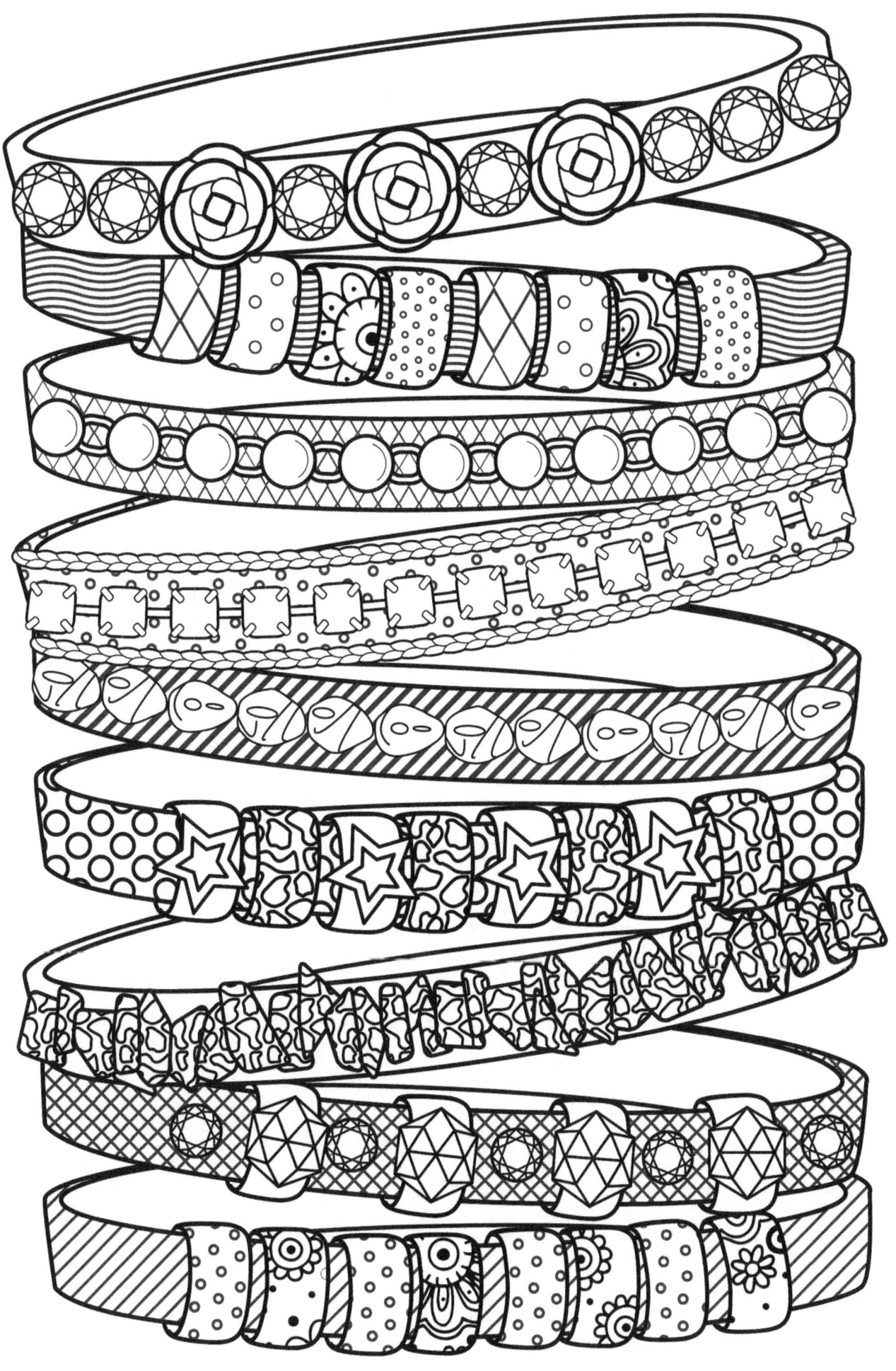

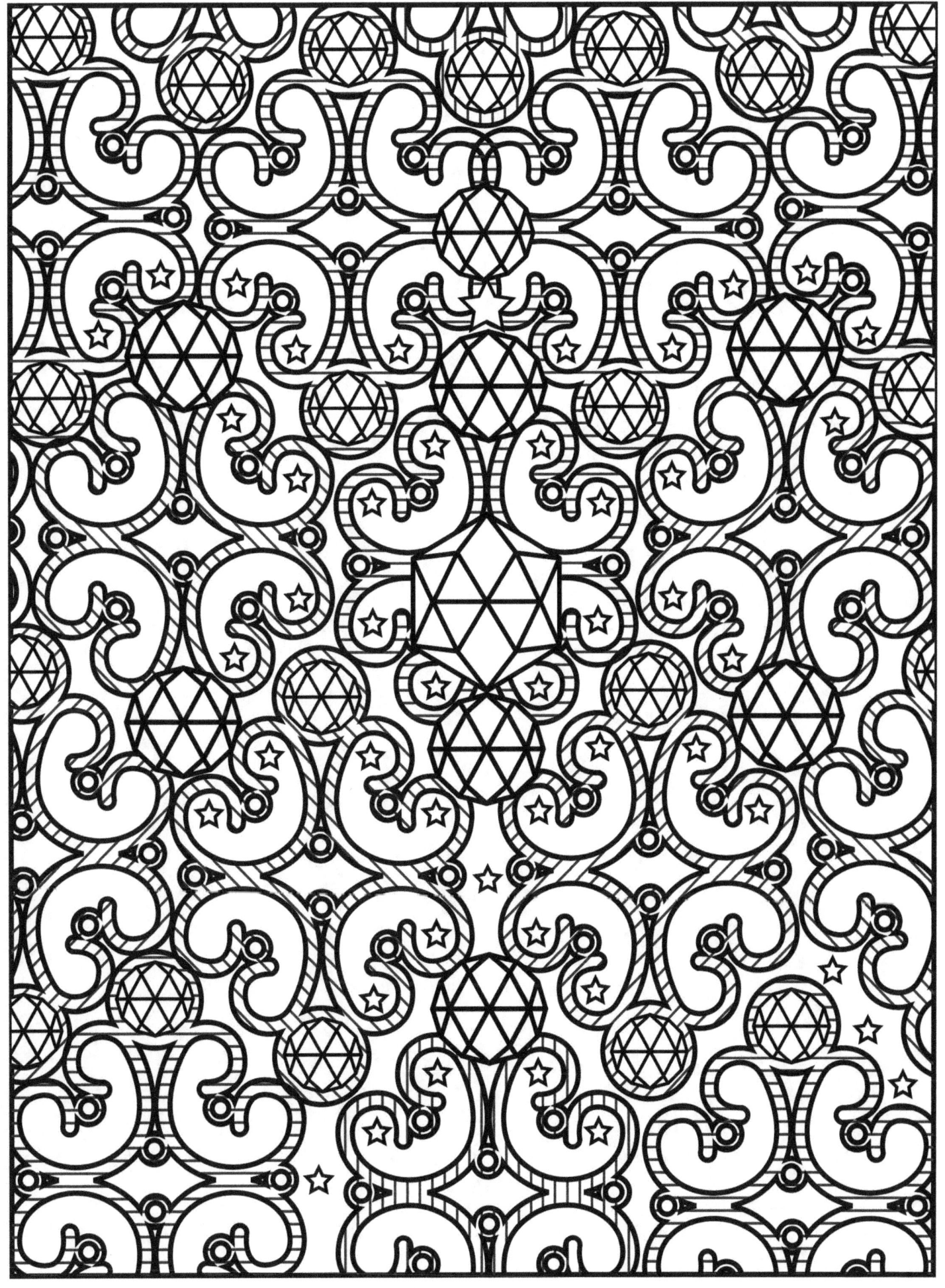

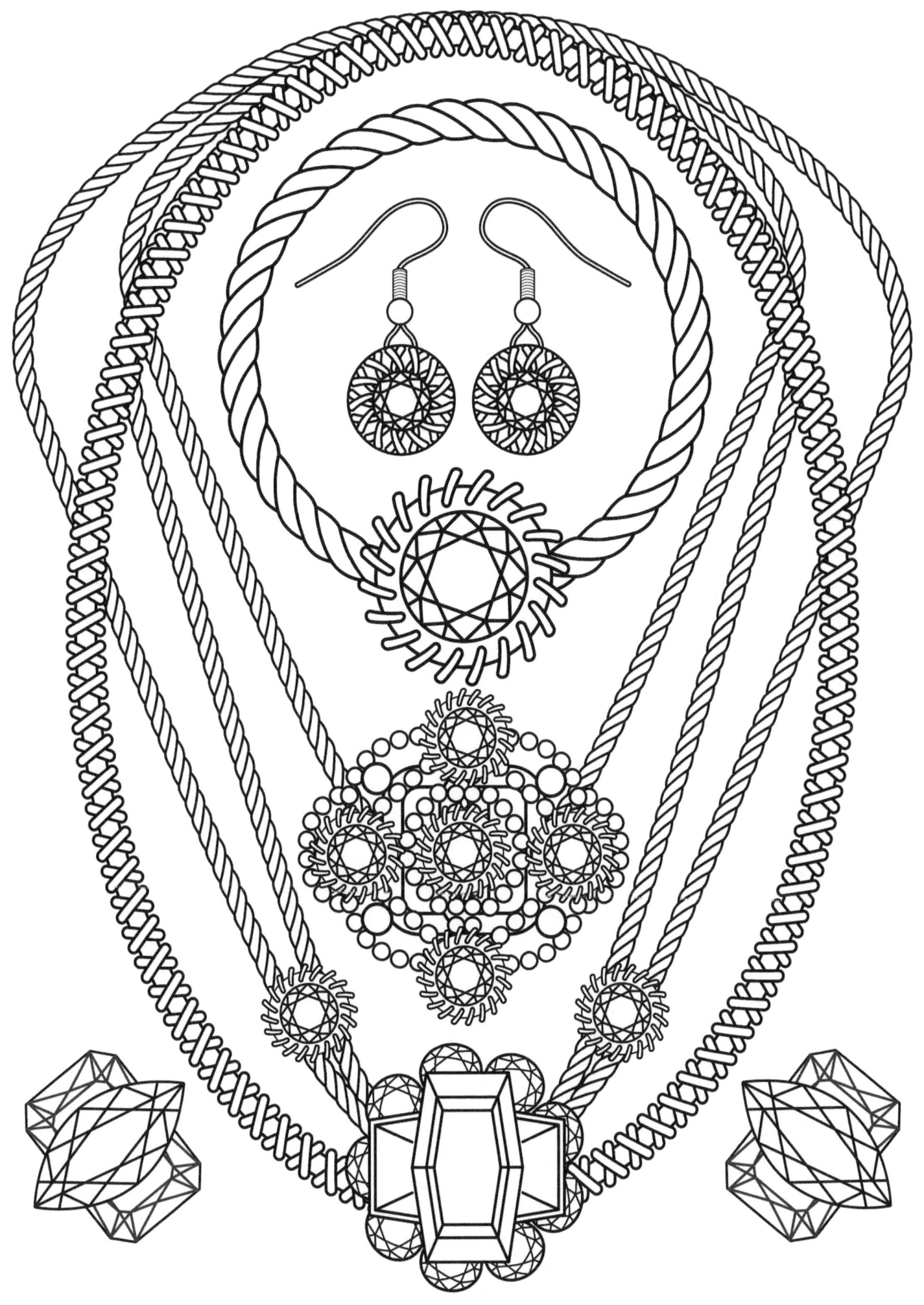

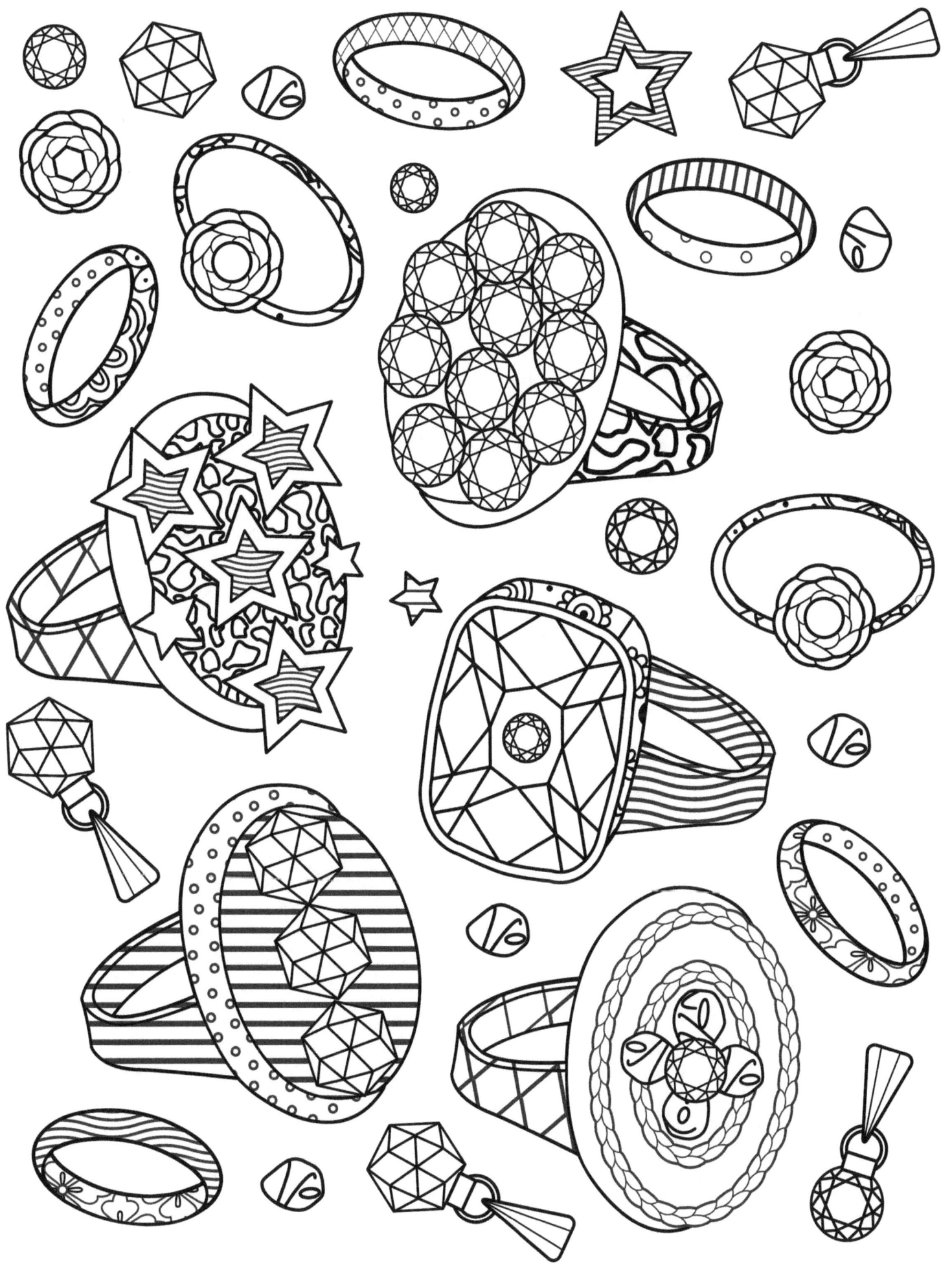

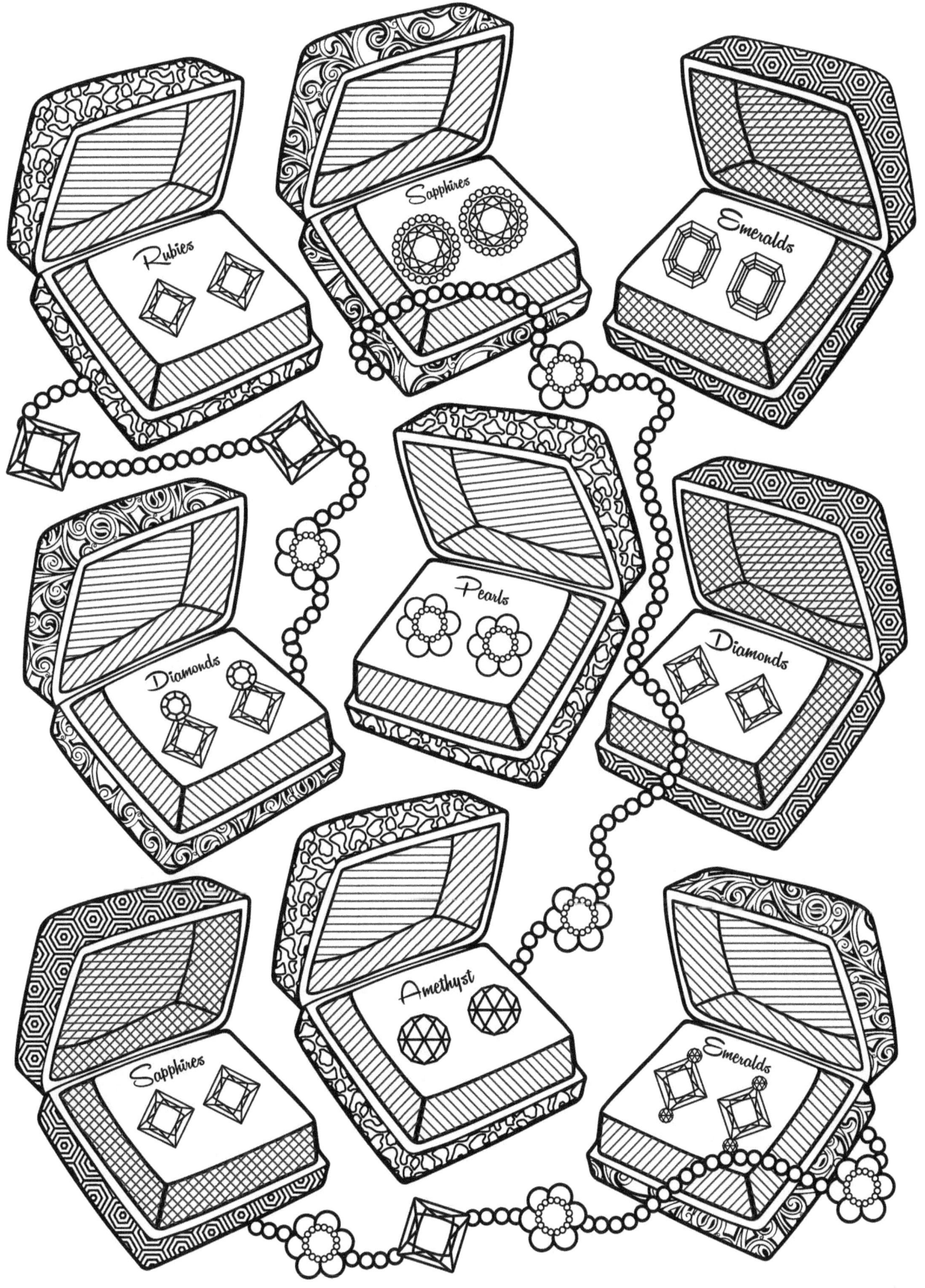

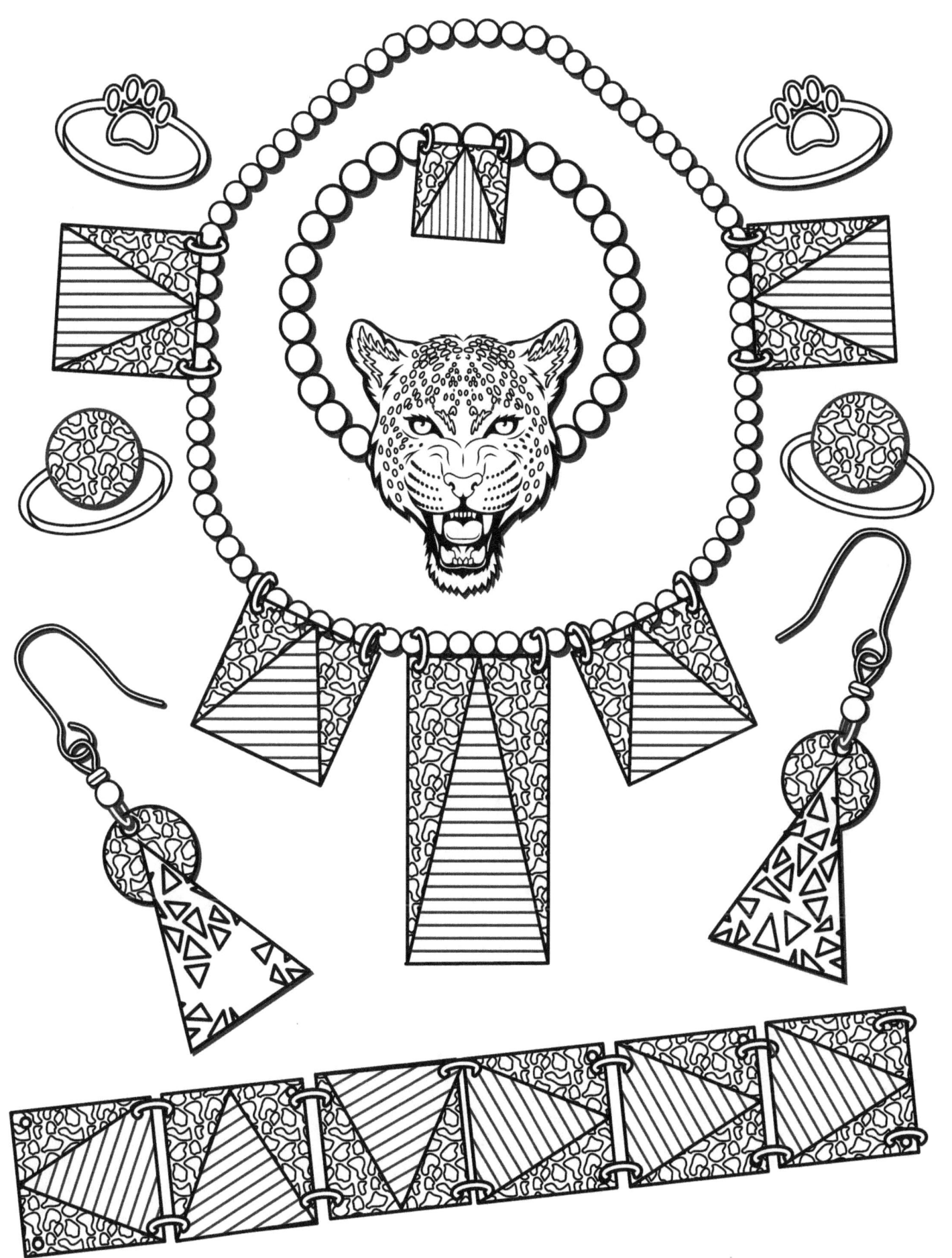

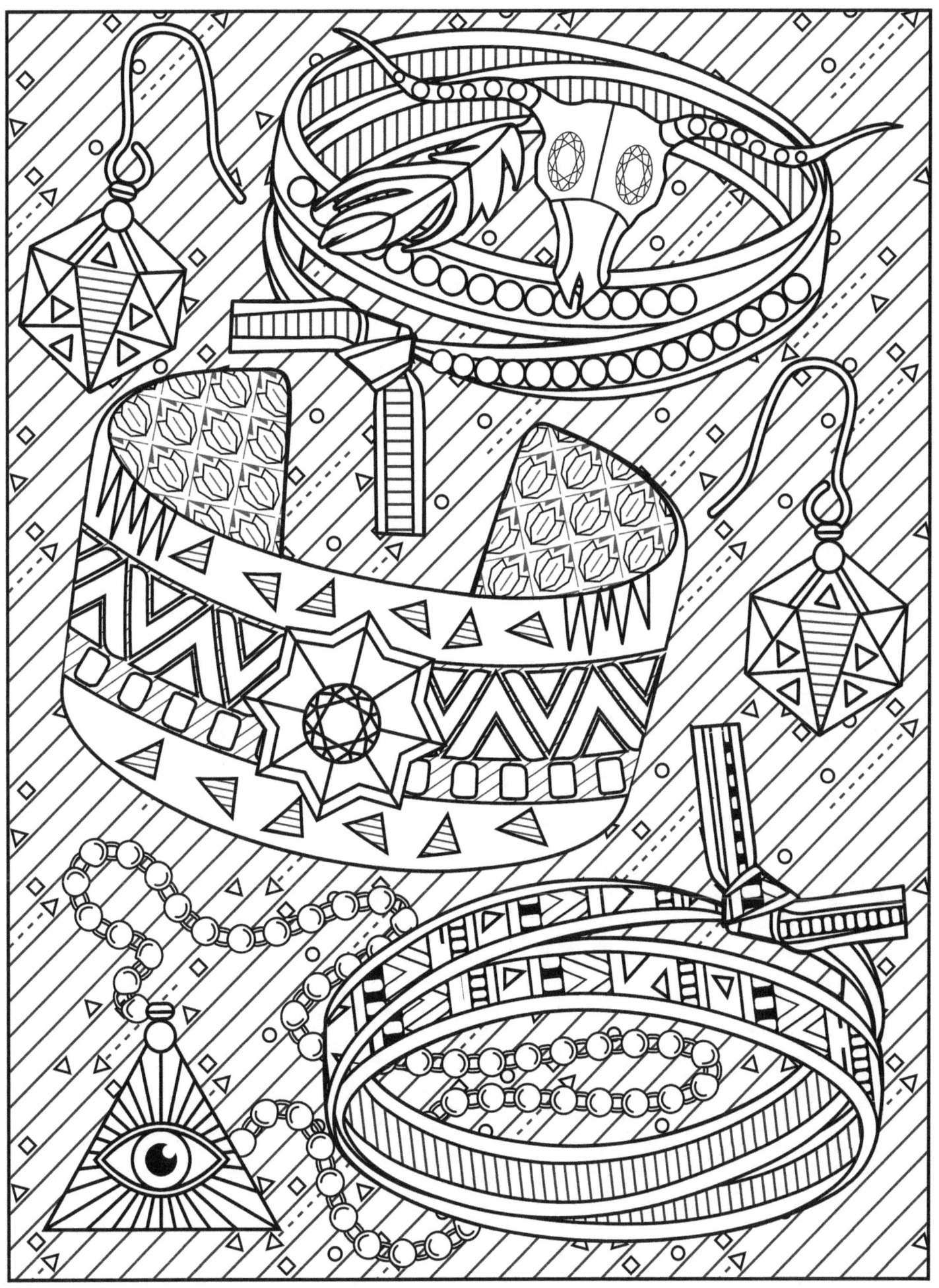

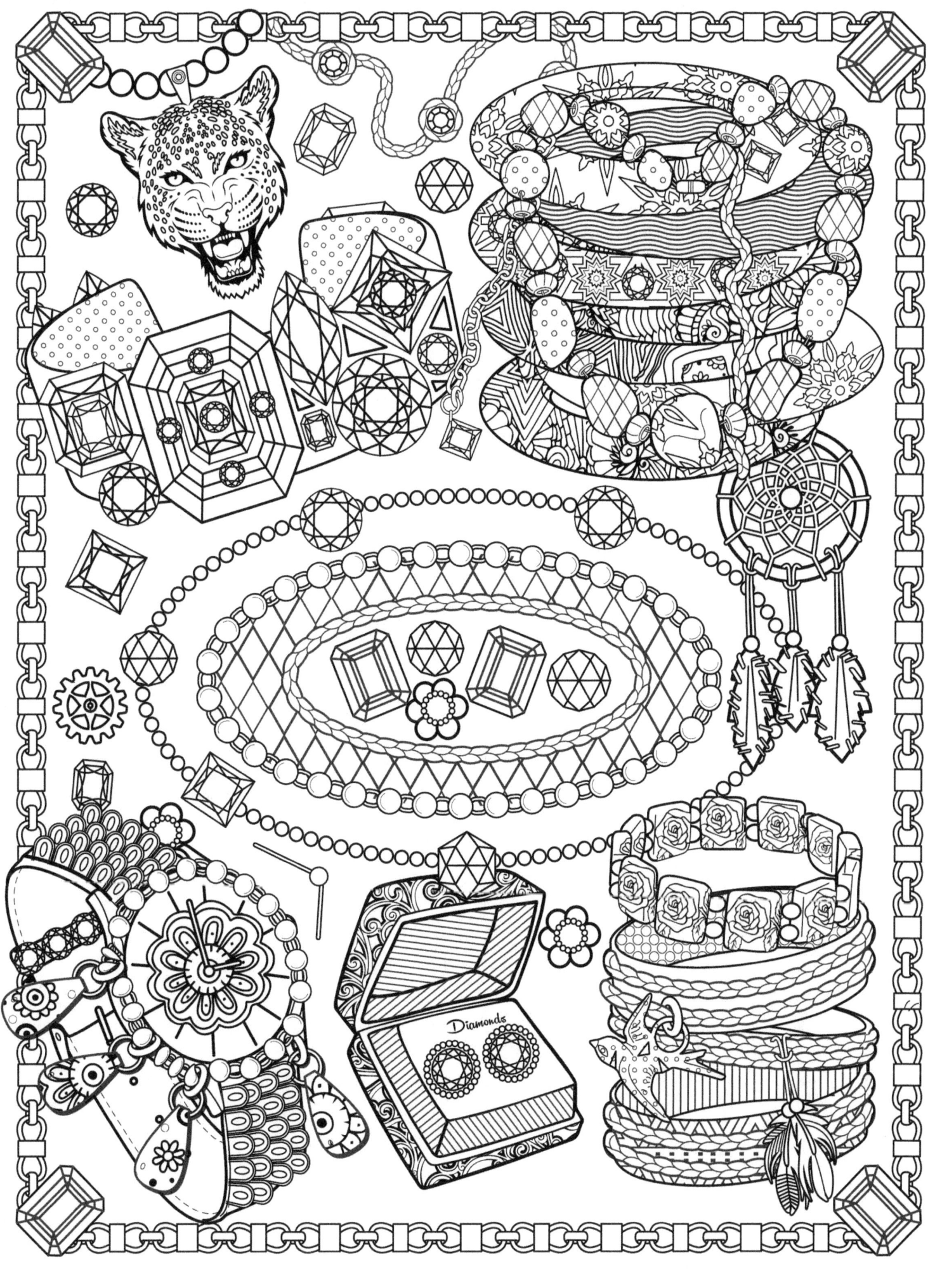

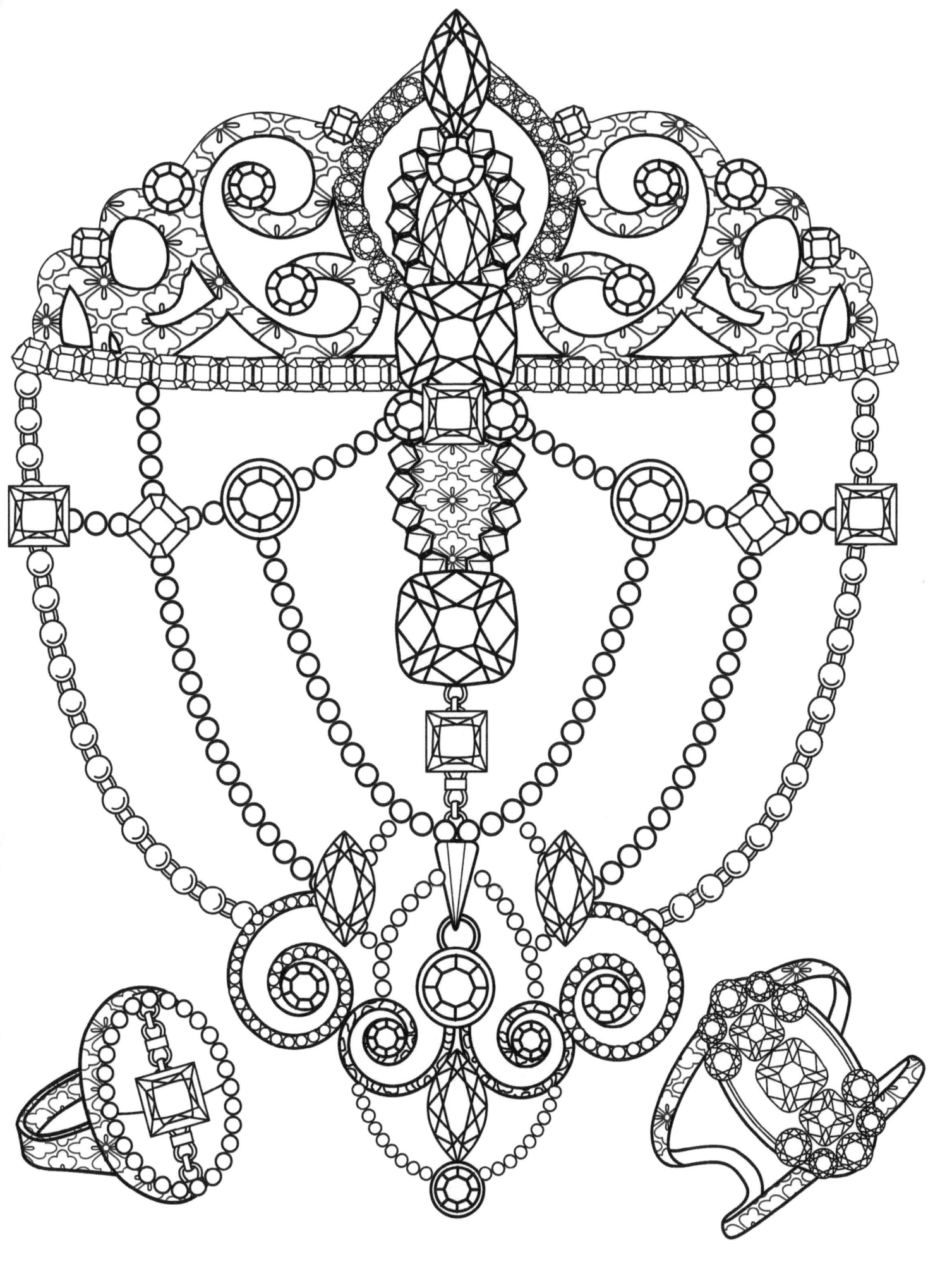

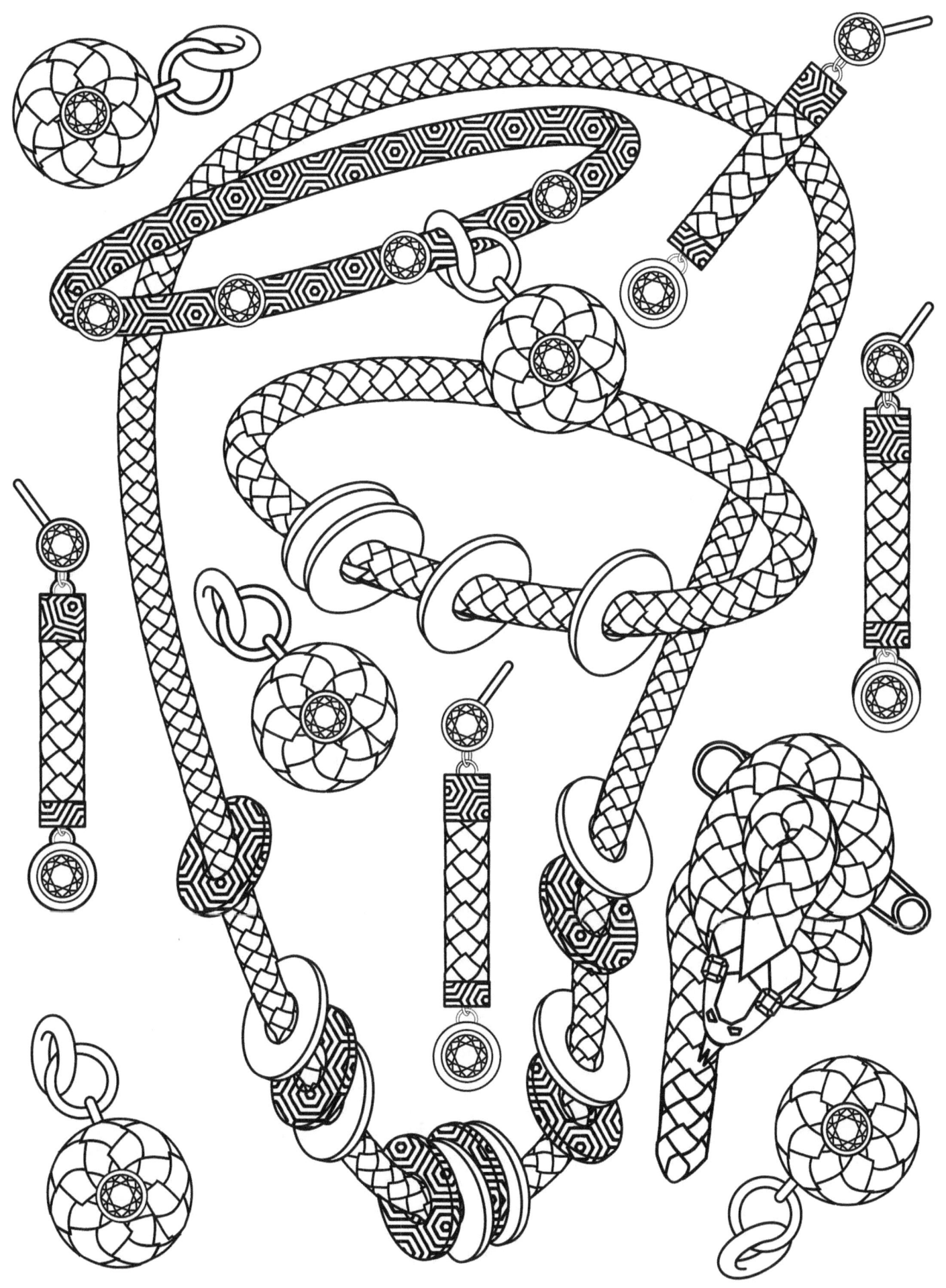

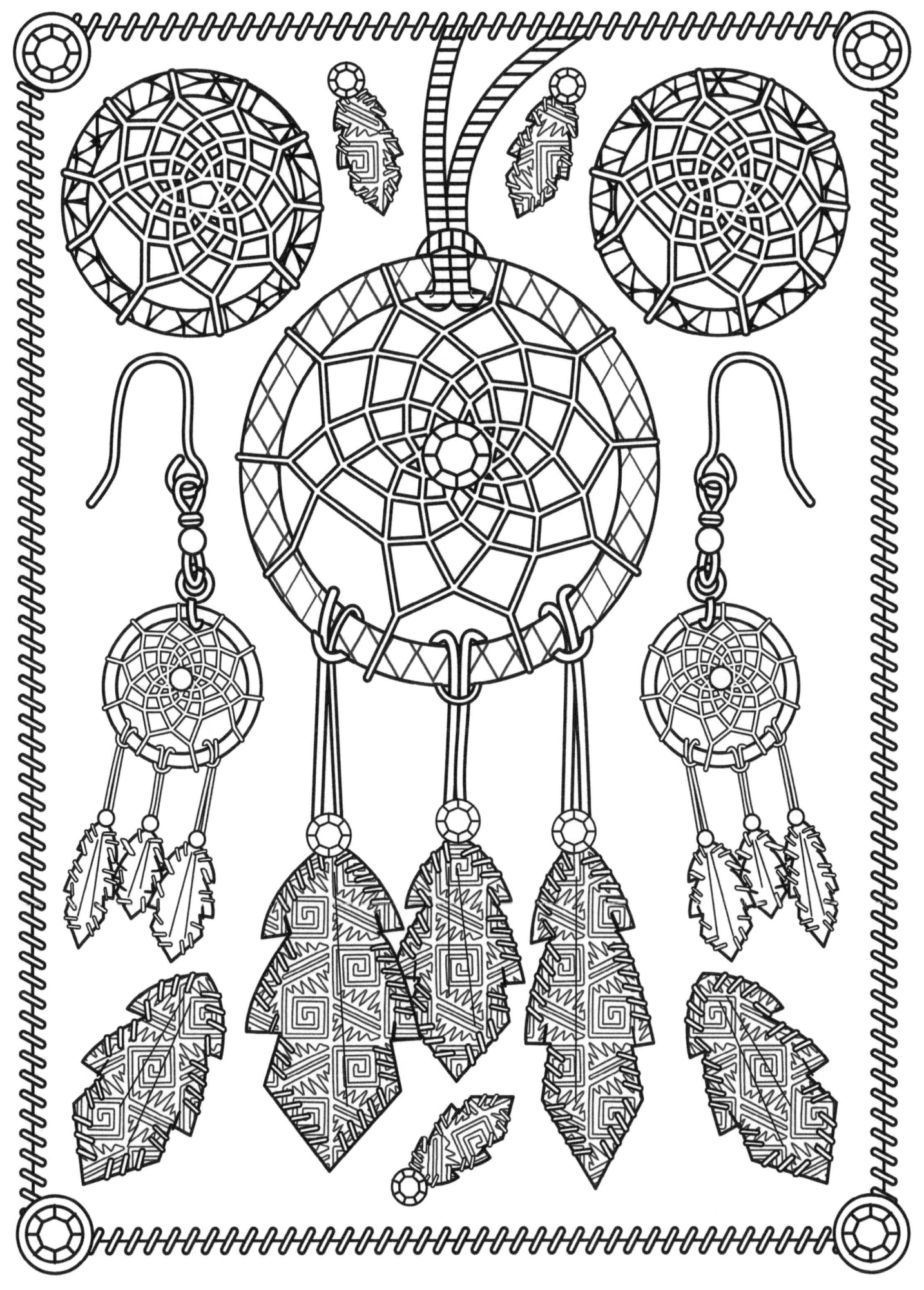

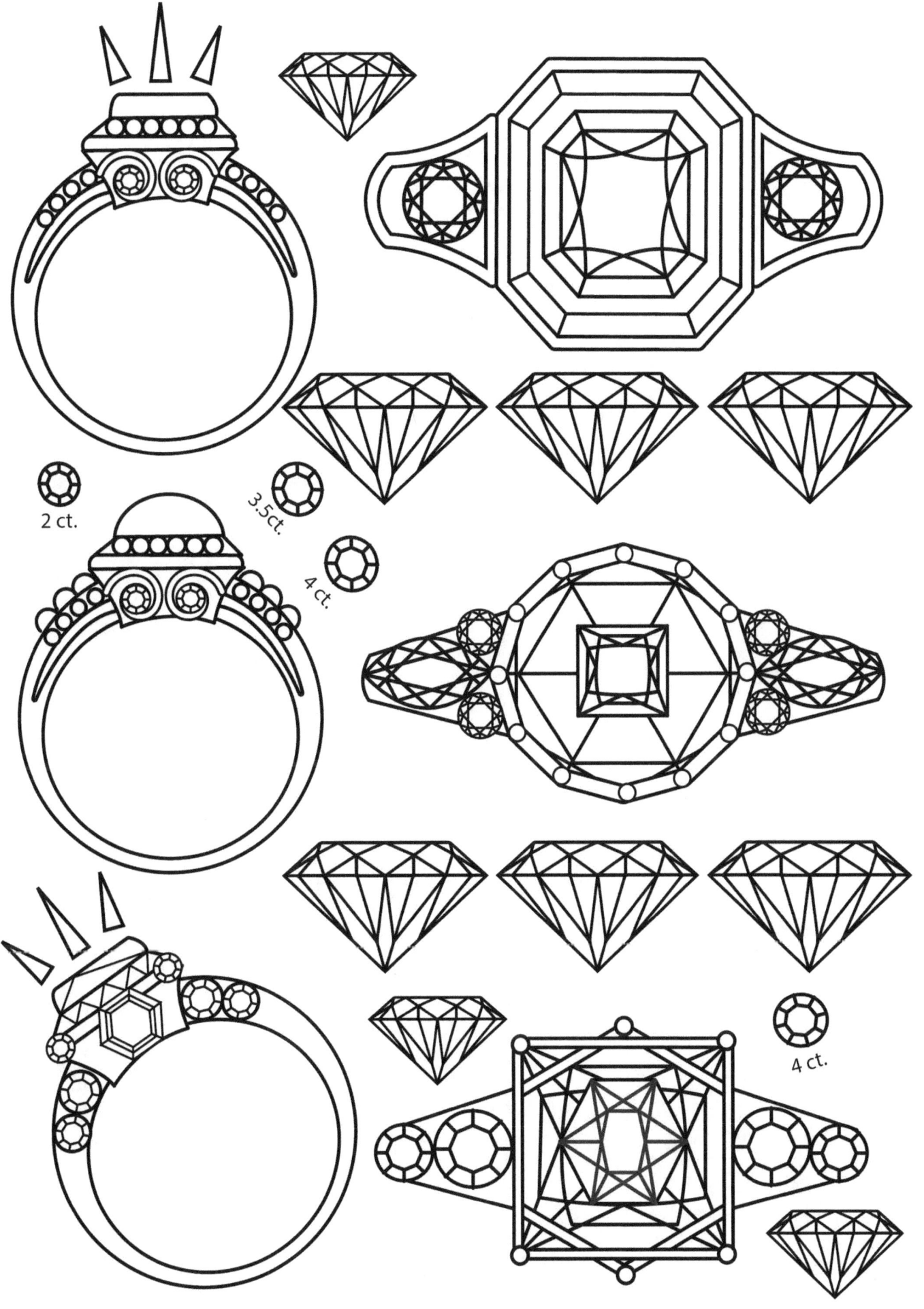

2 ct.

3.5 ct.

4 ct.

4 ct.

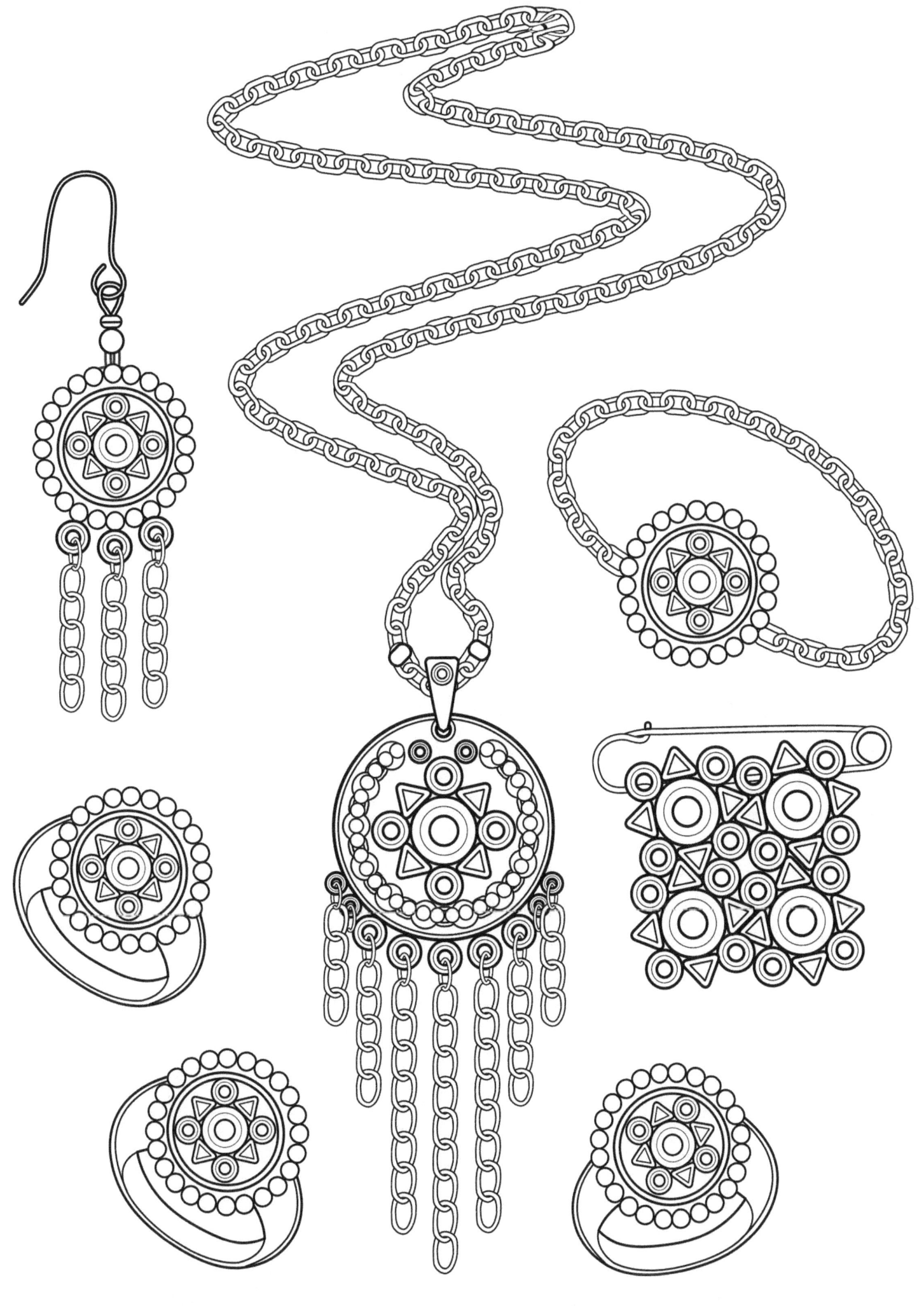

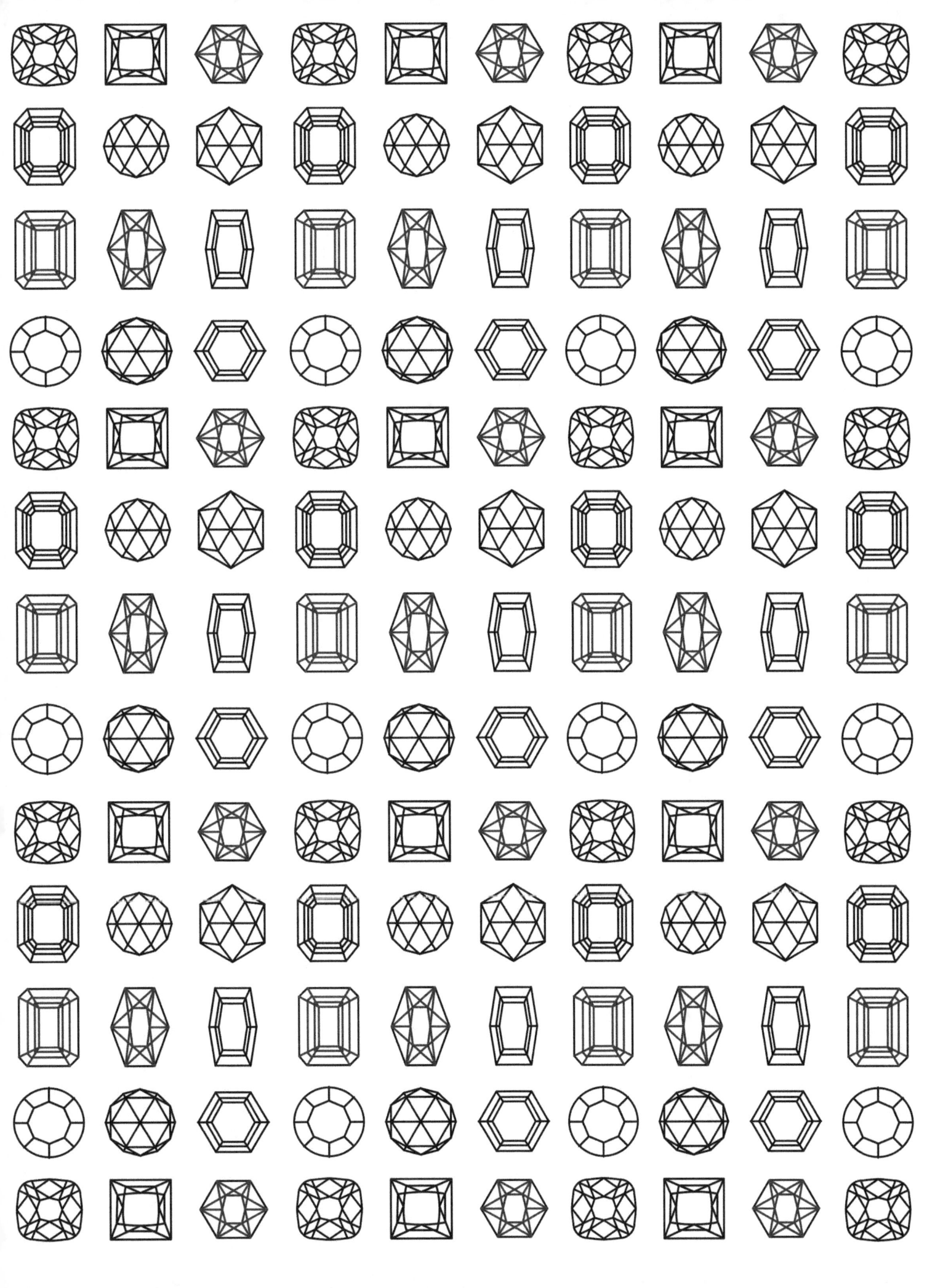

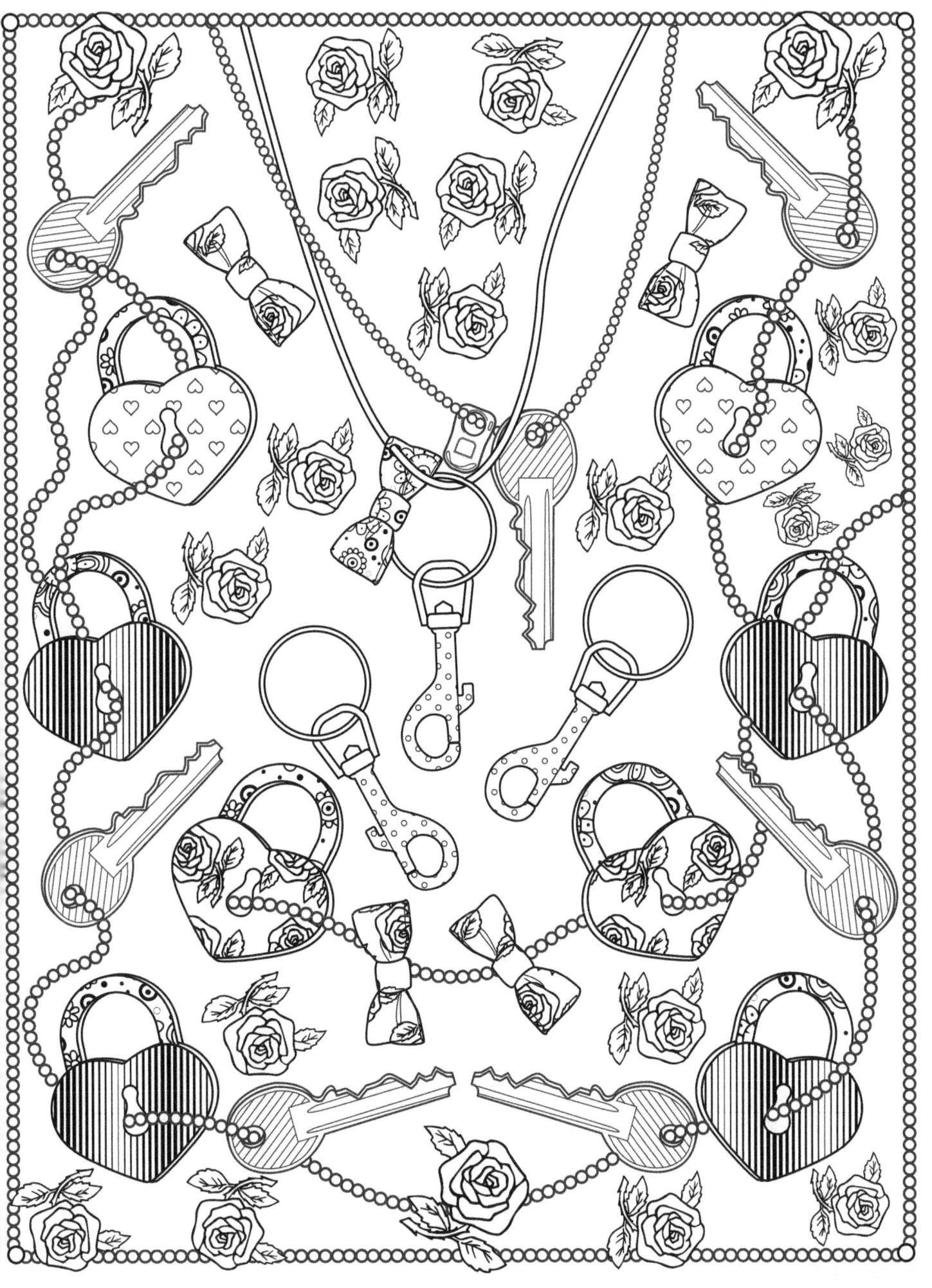